God is Justice

Are We in End Times?

Michael John DeNucci

Michael John DeNucci
Cumberland, WI

First Edition
June 2024
Printed in the United States
By http://thebookpatch.com
ISBN: 9798890904829

Acknowledgement

I thank the Holy Spirit for inspiring me to write this book.

Table of Contents

Table of Contents (cont.)

Preface

"Because the Lord is my Shepard, I have everything I need. He lets me rest in the meadow grass and leads me beside the quiet streams. He restores my failing health. He helps me do what honors him most.

Even when walking through the dark valley of death I will not be afraid, for you are close beside me, guarding, guiding all the way.

You provide delicious food for me in the presence of my enemies. You have welcomed me as your guest, blessings overflowing!

Your goodness and unfailing kindness shall be with me all of my life, and afterwards I will live… with you forever in your home." Psalm 23

Introduction

"Don't be afraid of those who can kill only your bodies—but can't touch your souls. Fear only God who can destroy both body and soul in hell. Not one sparrow (What do they cost? Two for a penny?) can fall to the ground without your Father knowing it. And the very hairs of your head are all numbered. So don't worry. You are more valuable to Him than many sparrows.

If anyone Publicly Acknowledges me as his Friend, I will openly acknowledge him as my Friend before my Father in Heaven (this refers to Jesus Christ and his heavenly father).

But, if anyone publicly Denies me, I will openly Deny him before my Father in heaven." Matt 10:28-33

1
Act of Love

Oh Lord, I Love You above all things with all my heart, soul and strength, and with Your help, I will Love my Neighbor as Myself.

2
My Mission in this Book

My mission in the book is to prepare persons for the Second Coming of Christ. My middle name—John— was given to me as named after John the Baptist who prepared persons for the First Coming of Christ. My mission is to prepare persons for the Second Coming of Christ.

My first name is Michael, named after Michael the Archangel. I imagine I am a protector against those who speak untruths. Even Donald J. Trump cannot escape the Truth. I view myself as a Spiritual Advisor to my fellow man.

Donald Trump was the Lawless One as the Anti-Christ is said to be in the Holy Bible (2:Thes:2:3-12) when he instigated the insurrection at the Capitol on January 6, 2021. Jesus Christ will come soon! Perhaps as the image of President Abraham Lincoln on His Chair at the Capitol in DC. saying: "What I have foretold has come True! (My words) What have you done to this country Donald? I tried to save this nation. You are destroying it for your own personal gratification. Shame on you!"

As who believe in Jesus Christ are his followers, so I am the brother of Jesus, the Son of God. Jesus lives through his spirit in each of us on Earth. Mary Magdalene was the first one to reach the tomb where the body of Jesus had been laid to rest. Jesus and Mary Magdalene were close friends. Jesus drove demons out of her and forgave her for adultery when faced by Jewish leaders who were preparing to stone her to death. Upon finding Jesus's body was not in the cave (tomb) Mary Magdalene ran to tell the Apostles that his body was not in the tomb.

I believe I have already personally experienced the Second Coming of Christ. I refer the reader to article 80 in my book Is God Happiness? Jesus: His Ascension into Heaven and His Second Coming:

"Jesus said before He ascended into Heaven in front of His Apostles: I will be with you until the end of time…You will see the Son of Man coming down from the sky just as you saw Him leaving. This points to Christ's Second Coming.

It could be He has already come to some of us in various ways. I heard a story about a hitchhiker who got in the back seat of a car and asked if the driver knew about the "Second Coming of Christ". When the driver turned to view the passenger hitchhiker, He had disappeared. I do not know if the story was true or not.

However, I had a similar experience many years ago with a "Helper" who flagged down a car for me, for I was out in a field after falling asleep and running off the road and unable to start my car. I did not know what to do when a person walking along the side of the highway smiled at me, so I walked up to Him and explained my situation. Then he flagged down a car for me and then instantly DISAPPEARED. When I got into the car, which He had flagged down, I looked back and there He was again, smiling at me. Was that Jesus? I do not know, but I believe it was at least an Angel. Whatever or Whoever you were, I do not believe I really thanked you until now" (as I write this book). Thank you to the person who helped me on that day!

Today, I believe that the "Helper" described in my book was Jesus. However, I believe that my experience of meeting Jesus was NOT what is described in 1 Thessalonians 4:15-18 "I can tell you this directly from the Lord: that you who are still living when the Lord returns will not rise to meet Him ahead of those who are in the graves. For the Lord Himself will come down from heaven with a mighty shout and with soul-stirring cry of the archangel and the great trumpet-call of God. And the believers who are dead will be first to rise to meet the Lord. Then we who are still alive and remain on earth will be caught up with them in the clouds to meet the lord in the air and remain with him forever. So, comfort and encourage each other with this news."

This "meeting the Lord in the air" for the believers still living is what is sometimes referred to as the RAPTURE. The Apostle's Creed reads: "He (Jesus) shall come to judge the living and the dead. So, I believe that Jesus' Second Coming will be what is called the Final Judgement or simply Judgement Day. On that day only those who are judged as being His faithful followers based on their Deeds will be lifted up into Heaven.

3
When Will Judgement Day Occur?

"I really don't need to say anything about that, dear brothers, for you know perfectly well that no one knows. That day of the Lord will come unexpected like a "thief in the night". When people are saying "All is well, everything is quiet and peaceful"—then, all of a sudden, disaster will fall upon them as suddenly as a woman's birth pains begin when her child is born. And these people will not be able to get away anywhere— there will be no place to hide."
1 Thessalonians 5:1-3

My interpretation of the preceding quote from St Paul in his first letter to the Thessalonians is there will be some great worldwide disaster or "tribulation"—probably nuclear war. We should be ready to meet Jesus at that time if we are still among the living. That is the time—end time—when only those true believers in Jesus Christ, as proven by their deeds, will meet Jesus in the

air and taken up into Heaven to be with Him, His Father, His Mother Mary and the Holy Spirit—the Rapture. But first those whose bodies and souls are in the graves will be judged by Jesus according to their deeds.

In conclusion, if we are Ready for Jesus all the time, he will invite us into Heaven. This is true concerning our deaths before the "great tribulation"—we who die before that occurs. Those believers dying before they experience their Second Coming of Christ will, I believe, be welcomed into Heaven, but possibly with some "purgatory" as refinement or education to prepare them for Heaven. Such purgatory has no suffering—certainly not the "fires of Hell." If we truly believe in Christ's promise of Everlasting Life, our souls will NOT

even go with our dead bodies into the grave —the
netherworld (hell) — when we die. Like the "good thief"
on the cross when Jesus was crucified and Jesus said
to him "This day you will be with me in paradise"—
Heaven. I refer the reader to articles 73 and 135 of my
book Is God Happiness? and articles 25 and 26 of my
book Happiness is the Truth.

4
Do We Trust God?

God's law is superior to man's law. One can be guilty
under man's law, while innocent under God's law.
Consider Jesus Christ when tried by the Jewish
leaders, which led to Christ's passion and death under
Jewish law as followed up under Roman Law. All of
Christ's apostles, except possibly John, were
reportedly killed when spreading Christianity. So they
were the first martyrs for Christ.

However, the first martyrs received their reward in the
afterlife and were canonized as Saints by the Roman
Catholic Church. God has the reward of Everlasting

Life and even Happiness on Earth to all of those who "follow" Jesus, though it may not immediately be apparent.

Jesus required that we Love God above all—with our whole heart, soul and strength—and that we love our neighbor as ourselves. We must love Our Neighbor to prove that we love God. The Bible states: "If anyone says, "I love God", but hates his brother, he is a liar". 1John 4:20. I interpret that today "brother" means everyone.

Trust God. Heaven awaits those who do so and prove it by following Jesus Christ's two commandments of LOVE: Love God with all your heart soul and mind and Love your neighbor as yourself. God is Justice!

5
Friendship with God: Does God Trust Us?

I view Jesus as a trusted friend. I believe He chose me to be His close friend. Also, I believe Jesus and I are Brothers. Based on this trust between us I must be humble to continue this trust relationship with Jesus. So, I should NOT try to "rise above it" for personal gain or be presumptuous.

We must all be humble to avoid the sin of presumption which is a state of arrogant assumption, which, in this case, would be presuming that we are going to heaven.

However, to trust completely in a solid friendship with Jesus, Who is God to the Earth, "weathering every storm" we CAN believe we are going to Heaven without presumption, but accepting Jesus Christ's promise of everlasting life through Faith in Him as proven by our deeds.

I must admit I have been presumptive in my belief concerning God. A woman once said to me "I answer to God". I replied: "I don't", meaning that Jesus is my friend and He trusts me, so I don't have to answer to Him. I was Wrong! We should answer especially to our closest friends.

They have that right to expect that. So, I abused Christ's friendship with me and took Him for granted, while He was and still is my Most important Friend. Answering to Him is expected now and when we meet Him in the afterlife when we will be held accountable to Him for what we did while living on earth. So, God trusted me, but I "let Him down" as we all do when we sin.

In conclusion, God Chose me by Loving me First. He had evidence that He could trust me by my acceptance of My Mission: "To Know, Love and Serve Him". I do this with my books and my example." (Art 11, My Mission in Life, my book Is God Happiness?). Also, God has answered my prayer: "Lord, make me an instrument of your Love, Peace and Inspiration to serve You and Others". (Art 97, My Prayer, my book Is God Happiness?) We must be Humble so that we do not "abuse" God's trust by taking it for granted. Justice requires that. God is Justice!

6
God Gives Us What We Need to be Happy

Some of our desires can be off God's path for us to be happy. God knows what we need. If we accept what he gives us, rather than complaining to him, we will be much happier. GOD GIVES US WHAT WE NEED, but NOT Necessarily what we Desire. Desires can be off God's path for us and lead us into much unhappiness. At times, we do not know if our desires are also needs. We will know the answer to that question by the way that God answers our prayer—either YES or NO. God gives us what we need, not just to physically survive, but to be happy in God's hands, for I have surrendered to God. I refer the reader to the old song: "He has the Whole World in His Hands" by Laurie London. You can find it on YouTube or perhaps another media you might have. Trust God! God is Justice!

7
Understanding

I have referred to President Joe Biden's letter to me in article 13 entitled: Understanding, in my book Is God Peace? Here is part of that letter from the White House signed by Joe Biden on June 3, 2021 after I had mailed him my first three books:

"Our country faces many challenges, but this is the time for Americans to set aside our differences to try to UNDERSTAND one another, and strive to make the promise of a just, prosperous and secure nation a reality for all". Note that he did NOT say "Let's make America great again" like the leading Republican presidential candidate has said. To me American is still great. Listen to the song "Americana" sung by Moe Bandy, a country singer. Try YouTube or whatever media you have. It talks of "small town America" which is where I live—Cumberland, Wisconsin, population 2274. The song say's "I found so many reasons why I love this country. "America is still safe and sound". Let's keep it that way. No politician is completely honest in every detail, but Joe Biden is not just a politician, but a true statesman who came up through the ranks and wants to represent ALL Americans with Integrity. He has won my respect. I hope he can win yours.

Finally, continuing with article 13 of my book Is God Peace?: "Understanding help promote Peace. It is the second gift of the Holy Spirit. So, God, through the

Holy Spirit grants us Understanding leading us to Peace. God is Peace" and Justice!

8
"Put Your Hand in the Hand"

The title of this article refers to the song "Put Your Hand in the Hand" first sung by Anne Murray and written by Gene McClellan was a gospel pop song. It says: "Put you hand in the hand of the man from Galilee. Put your hand in the hand of the man who calms the sea....When I read the Holy book I want to tremble. Look at yourself and you may see others differently, for we aren't the people we want to be...". Thus the need for repentance.

I refer the reader to my book Is Love the Truth? Article 13, "Compromise Based on the Truth".

"The truth is not relative. Something is either "true" or it is not. Sit down and talk with your opponent, if that's how you view him/her, until you both feel at ease to discuss issues...listen, rather than just saying "no", and then stating your opinion. Think: could there be something that is true in what the other person is saying? That is NOT selling out. Minds can and should change at times. If we do not listen and compromise, we are stuck in the polarization that has occurred and stymied our government ...let's change. God knows we need to! Love is the Truth!"

Referring back to the song: "Put your hand in the hand", if we realize that Jesus, who is the focus of the song, spoke the Truth and some politicians are persistent liars, we certainly CAN and SHOULD admit our error of supporting the wrong candidates if we have done so. Admitting we were wrong takes humility and courage. However, our nation will be better off as well as the whole world if we do so. The United States of America is still the Beacon of Hope for Freedom for the whole world. With Governments of Communist nations having little moral compass and takes actions benefiting only their own people, the U.S.A. tends to care about all peoples of the world like in the song currently playing on my I-pad through YouTube "We are the World" featuring big singing stars in the benefit for Africa. It states: "We are the ones who will make a brighter day, so let's start giving...We're saving our own lives." (Produced by Quincy Jones, written by Lionel Richie and Michael Jackson, and sung by Bob Dylan, Diana Ross, Cindi Lauper, Stevie Wonder, Kenny Rogers and others.). We are all connected today.

So "put your hand in the hand of the Man from Galilee" —Jesus Christ- and LOVE ONE ANOTHER as He has loved us. There is a Price to Pay for NOT doing so. God is Justice!

9
Preventing Misunderstandings

I refer the reader back to art 7 in this book. TRY to Understand others to Prevent Misunderstandings so that we are led to Peace and Prevent War. This includes Understanding at the Domestic level as well as the International level.

International Relations should center around diplomacy first rather than military action, which should be a last resort. FEAR often leads to Hatred, which results in Misunderstandings.. I refer the reader to my book Is God Happiness? art 33, Fear and Hatred. "There are times when unfounded fear can lead to hatred. People can be so afraid of something or someone that they turn to Hate and try to Destroy that fear by damaging or destroying that which they conceive as the source of that fear. Only Love can destroy fear if we do not want to destroy people or take away their freedom. And we should Never want to destroy people or even take away their freedom if we can use diplomacy which can lead to Love. This applies to both personal and international relations. (Of course, self-defense and national defense including defense of our allies are OK and even necessary at times when attacked by others."

I refer the reader to my book Is God Happiness? art 108, Forgiveness and Trust: Hope for Mankind. "Unless people turn to God for forgiveness, it is difficult for them to turn to others for forgiveness after offending them...On a larger scale, mankind has waged war since the beginning of recorded history...Nations should try to forgive each other to move forward with Peace and Love. Hatred and revenge too often result in war. The extreme damage of war was exemplified by the atomic bombing of Hiroshima and Nagasaki which ended World War Two with Japan. I do not claim to judge the morality of those final attacks, but it clearly showed us the dangers of Nuclear War. Trust built on Love and Truth is the cement that can hold mankind together to avoid war if we possibly can. Practice diplomacy if possible. It is our hope for peace, if we can do it."

Violence is too often the result of misunderstandings. The virtue of Patience is necessary to "hear" another's side of an issue before turning to hateful attacks due to unfounded fear. Exhaust all means to legitimately Keep the Peace. However, do not settle for Peace at any Cost, but realize that the Truth should Never be jeopardized simply to keep the Peace. I refer the reader to my book *Is God Peace?,* art 12, *Should We Remain Silent to Keep the Peace?* "At times I have remained imprudently silent by "going along with some action" in order to "keep the peace". However, we have an obligation to "speak up" when our better judgment tells us to do so. One could even say speak up "when the spirit moves us". It could be the Holy Spirit inspiring us to prevent an injustice."

In conclusion, patiently practice Love which can prevent misunderstandings which too often lead to violent actions, either concerning unjust "freedom restrictions" for persons or nations, or violent acts and, at times, losing a "good relationship" with someone or, internationally, a "good Ally". The United States of American is the only nation on earth to ever have used nuclear weapons. Let's hope and pray such weapons are Never used again and that all other nations of the world develop a "healthy" respect for us, the USA, if they do not already have it. Justice requires such a Healthy Respect. God is Justice!

10
Eve of Destruction

The song Eve of Destruction written by P.F. Sloan and Steve Barri and sung by Barry McGuire in 1965 and by others was a protest song against injustices of that era, especially in the context of the Vietnam War. Its release was shortly after the United States entered the

Vietnam War, (Gulf of Tonkin Resolution, Aug 7 1964).
Our initial mission was to use any means necessary to
restore international peace and security to Southeast
Asia. The war pitted the United Staes, Australia, New
Zealand, Republic of (South) Korea, Thailand and the
Philippines against the North Vietnamese Army, the
"NVA", the Peoples's Army of Vietnam and the
People's Liberation Armed Forces of South Vietnam.
Collectively they were called the Viet Cong by the
United States.

The song Eve of Destruction speaks of injustices and
hypocrisy. I refer the reader to art 4 of this book, Do
We Trust God? "If anyone says, I love God, but hates
his brother, he is a liar" 1 John: 4:20. I interpret that
today "brother" means everyone. Jesus repeatedly
warned the Jewish leaders not to be hypocrites. The
result of such warning and criticism resulted in the
UNJUST crucifying of Jesus by the Jewish leaders
under Roman law. Christ's message was Love—Love
God above all and Love your Neighbor as yourself. His
words and miracles were so powerful that those Jewish
leaders feared he would become more influential than
themselves. So, it was both fear and jealousy that led

to Jesus Christ's passion and death. But he was Resurrected by his Heavenly Father and will come back to "judge the living and the dead". (Apostles' Creed).

In conclusion, the song Eve of Destruction justifiably warns of nuclear holocaust. However, do NOT fear what we cannot control. Do not fear death, because God is watching over those He loves. (I refer the reader back to the Preface and Introduction to this book.) If nuclear war does occur in our lifetime, remember that Jesus Christ Himself will return on Judgement Day "like a thief in the night", unexpectedly, to take all of His Believers to Heaven with Him and leave all the evil unbelievers to punishment bought on by their own hate and disrespect for Life. The entire Bible (New American, revised, St Joseph Edition) ends with these words: "Yes, I am Coming soon".
Amen! The grace of our Lord Jesus be with you all."
Revelations, Chapter 22, verses 20-21

11
Sweet Cherry Wine

The above title refers to the song from 1969 sung by Tommy James and the Shondells, written by Richard Grasso and Tommy James and produced by Tommy James. The song is an anti-war song. It talks of drinking sweet cherry wine rather than going to war.

From Wikipedia I found this:

"James, in an interview on the Christian Broadcasting Network (CBN) in 2010 stated that the song "was about the blood of Jesus" and acknowledged that many fans and peers assumed it was drug related". It is also a protest song about the Vietnam War."

Tommy James' music was considered by some as psychedelic at that time. Thus, the drug relationship inferred by some. It also spoke of the value of drinking sweet wine and to "get together" feeling "good" from the effects of the wine. It implied that if people "feel good" they are less likely to succumb to Anger leading to fighting as in War. One the contrary, such an activity of "intoxication" can remove anger and get people "together".

In my opinion, if people want Peace through bringing people together through alcoholic drinks, such behavior is Virtuous and helps to prevent war. Such activity can lead to a Love Relationship between important world leaders who might decide that the other "Nation" who we had thought was our enemy is truly our friend. This bonding can be expressed with hugging, with or without alcoholic drinks, such as between President Richard Nixon and General Secretary of the Communist Party Leonid Brezhnev when Nixon was President. I believe President Trump also made an attempt at Love with Kim, the leader of North Korea, but I believe his attempt has failed with North Korea recently testing a missile reportedly capable of striking anywhere in the U.S. mainland.

Finally, getting back to the song Sweet Cherry Wine, James said it referred to the "blood of Jesus". The Catholic Church and the Missouri Synod of the Lutheran Church believe that the wine which they normally drank at certain services is the Physical Blood of Jesus. (Refer to me book Fishing for Heaven, art 4, Jesus Everlasting Life). Other Protestant churches and, I believe, some non-denominational Christian churches believe it is only a Symbol of His Blood as a commemoration of the Last Supper.

In conclusion, there are dangers of drinking too much "sweet wine"—liver damage, behavioral issues, etc. However, when weighed against the dangers of War, drinking wine seems less dangerous to me. The song Sweet Cherry Wine was a Protest against the Vietnam War. That war was unjust. However, the Cause was just— preventing the spread of Communism. But, we had almost no chance of winning that war because our soldiers did Not know enough about the will of our enemies to protect their homeland through jungle warfare, rice paddies warfare, and our military personnel not recognizing persons without uniforms as to who was our enemies versus our allies whom we were trying to defend against the Viet Cong as backed by Communist China. The Catholic Church taught in the 1960s that if we cannot expect success in any war, it is Unjust and results in a needless number of deaths. The Vietnam Conflict Data File of the Defense Casualty

Analysis System Extract Files contains records of 58,220 U.S. military fatalities casualties of the Vietnam War. Also, an estimated 2 million Asian civilians died due to that war. (National Archives, Encyclopedia Britannia).

When Richard Nixon was in office he bombed the North Korean Capital—Hanoi. I once read more bombs were dropped on Hanoi than all bombs dropped by the U.S. on Germany during World War Two. I believe Nixon did this to "bring North Vietnam to its knees" as President Truman did with two Atomic Bombs to end World War Two with Japan. (Nixon dropped only conventional bombs—not Atomic or Nuclear).

A successful attempt to end U.S involvement in the war was made in Paris, France with the Paris Peace Accord on January,1973. However, the accord was broken with resumed fighting between North and South Vietnam. The US officially pulled out all troops in 1975 with the fall of Saigon when on April 30, Communist forces captured the presidential palace in Saigon, ending the Second Indochina War. So, the United

States LOST the Vietnam War after more than 58,000 U.S. deaths due to fighting that war. What eventually resulted was unification of North and South Vietnam under a Communist Party. It is estimated that about 1.1 million Viet Cong combatants lives were lost. Also, during the conflict, an estimated 2 million civilian deaths occurred in North and South Vietnam, Laos and Cambodia. (Some estimated that 1.2 million were murders.).

In conclusion, "War is Hell". A co-worker in the Vista Program, when I was in non-military Federal volunteer work, made that statement to me after he had been an officer in Vietnam during the Vietnam War.

War is Hell! Let's stay out of War as much as we can. Better to have a glass of "Sweet Cherry Wine" and discuss the issues.

Jesus was referred to as a "drunk" by some of the "Pharisees and scholars of the law "who were not baptized by John the Baptist and rejected the plan of God for themselves." Luke 7:30 "for John the Baptist came neither eating food nor drinking wine...The Son of Man (Jesus) came eating and drinking and you (Pharisees and scholars of the law) said, Look, he (Jesus) is a glutton and a drunk." Luke 7:33-34. Jesus spoke of the two new Commandments, which are the basis of the whole Law (especially the Ten Commandments): "You shall love the Lord, your God with all your heart, with all your soul and with all you mind. This is the greatest and the first commandment: The second is similar. You shall love your neighbor as yourself. The whole law and the prophets depend on these two commandments."

I refer the reader to my book Is God Peace? Article 23, One Tin Soldier. The article refers to the song One Tin Soldier sung by Coven and written by Bryan Potter and Dennis Lampert. The song is very anti-war. The article in my book ends like this:

"With nuclear arsenals more than enough to destroy mankind many times over, War is NOT the answer; not like it was thought it be with the Crusades between the Christians and the Moslems between 1096 AD and 1291 AD or more recently the Terrorist attack by radical Moslems on our nation on 9/11/2001.

Christ's PEACE is more important than any Holy War fought in His name. May the PEACE of Christ bring us to PEACE, NOT WAR! Love is all that matters! Love Rules! The TWO COMMANDMENTS of LOVE from JESUS RULE OUT WAR!"

So, I repeat: share a glass of sweet cherry wine or beer or any drink, alcoholic or nonalcoholic, with one another and DISCUSS the ISSUES! Discuss the issues anywhere people come together. Even the Bars! Even to discuss Religion and Politics! Jesus said: Wherever two or more are gathered in My Name, I will be there with them. This "Place should NOT be only in Churches! I refer the reader to my book *Is Love the Truth?* article 29, "Do We Ever Feel Almost Like A "Fool" For Jesus" and article 33, When and Where is the Right Time to Talk about God?" Justice and World Peace depend on such discussions. God is Justice!

12
What is Love?

Love is wishing well to another and proving it by offering good deeds or gifts or anything beneficial to another. Though many persons associate Love as some undefined dream, that type of love is romantic love which can lead one to express it strongly with significant help to the one of his/her dreams. Such love is what happens when one "falls in love" and it is based on feelings one has for another. If one "lets his/her guard down" for one with whom he/she is attracted, usually physically attracted, romantic love is usually the result.

However, romantic love is often difficult to continue if the object of such romance becomes less physically attractive. For example, if one gets "fat", "wrinkles up" in the face or other forms of becoming less physically attractive. I find the eyes are important in physical attraction.

But, in conclusion, one's love for another is proven after romantic love dies or greatly diminishes if one's love for the other continues as AN ACT of the WILL which still requires wishing well for another and "doing things" for the benefit of the other. Love is NOT a myth. Love can be attained and preserved if one perseveres with determination to have a successful "love relationship". Such love is found in many long-term marriages which is a result of "climbing over obstacles" rather than simply taking the easier path of "going around the obstacles" and separating or divorcing the other person in the relationship. Such separations often lead to instability of the society especially if children are "victims" of the separation. To "discard" another after one has no use for him/her with no regard for the wellbeing of the other is immoral. Justice requires one to persevere in love. God is Justice!

13
The Right to Life: Contraception or Abortion?

My answer to the above question comes to me very easily. Which is better: to prevent an unwanted baby from forming in a woman's womb through contraception OR allowing an unwanted baby to be formed only to be faced with the decision whether to abort that human life in her womb after conception. It is a NO BRAINER to me! Use Contraception!

My understanding of the Catholic Church's opposition to contraception is that it interferes with the NATURAL reproductive process in a woman. I admit that it does. However, I believe my answer is still a valid decision. Just look around. How many families that we know have 8 or more children today? I believe the answer is NOT many. So most use Contraception—even Catholics. The acceptable rhythm method is too inconvenient, in my opinion. Timing when a couple wants to "make love" and have sexual intercourse is unpredictable and planning for the event ruins the joy of spontaneity. So, I believe few Catholic couples follow the Catholic Church's position on Contraception. Come on Catholic Church leaders! Let's move out of the "dark ages" which was when the Catholic Church wanted MORE CATHOLICS to populate the earth and the contraception pill was not available yet. Let's have more Quality Catholics—those who practice LOVE as

Jesus commands. I might add, we do not need more SNOBS, "better than thou" persons of any religious sect. They are like the Pharisees in Jesus' time.

Finally, my position on abortion is a very firm belief. I believe in the RIGHT to LIFE! I refer the reader to article 36 in my book Is God the Truth? entitled "Do We React to Only Those with a Voice?"

I am an "attorney" who defends Jesus Christ— a "freelance writer for God and Mankind", as noted with my photo near the end of this book and all my books. As noted near the beginning of this book in Acknowledgements, I am inspired by the Holy Spirit.

14
Make America Great Again? Revolution? Civil War?

Some persons in our Great nation believe that conditions are so terrible that we need to go backwards to make America great again. To those persons, we need a military-like Revolution or Civil War to make Donald J Trump our President. He instigated the insurrection at our Capitol. I recall a man violently breaking into the Capitol saying "We're listening to your President." That President was Donald J. Trump on January 6, 2021 and it was displayed on major TV networks.

Some say it was a conspiracy by Democrats to fool the public. As their argument unfolds, they claim that Democrats placed "fake" persons at the insurrection to make people believe that the Republicans were behind the insurrection.

Another argument goes like this: the Capitol police voluntarily let violent people into the building to make it look like the Capitol police were the culprits. What I saw on TV was a Capitol policeman leading some of those who had broken into the building. He led them down a hallway. A news commentator explained that the policeman led them intentionally down the wrong hallway so that some members of Congress could escape through another hallway.

I watched a Capitol policeman being physically hurt while trying to protect those congressmen and women in the Capitol building. The conspiracy theory used by Trump supporters would say it was persons backed by the Democrats who hurt that police officer. Also, Jake Tapper of CNN said to TV viewers and listeners that some dead bodies were found in the Capitol building. This I confirmed on Wikipedia.

This conspiracy theory spawns one argument after another to get Donald J. Trump re-elected. So, is this the plan? Let's have a Revolutionary War or Civil War to get Donald J. Trump re-elected because only he can solve all the world's problems. Such thinking leads to this conclusion: just listen to what Trump says he wants and follow his directives because the United States of America needs an "outsider with No prior experience in government before his first term as President, but someone who is a successful businessman who "knows how to make money". Their thinking is that ALL politicians are corrupt. To me, Donald J. Trump is the prime example of a corrupt politician. Trump lied to get the Presidency back. He is a salesman only for Himself, not a statesman, like

Biden. He appeals to only his followers. He does NOT represent All Americans. I refer you to article 7 of this book entitled Understanding in which I quote President Biden from a letter he mailed me on June 3, 2021 from the White House signed by Joe Biden: "Our country faces many challenges, but this is the time for Americans to set aside our differences, to try to understand one another, and to strive to make the promise of a just, prosperous, and secure Nation a reality for all." I believe that Trump wanted to be "King" of the United States of America, not just a duly elected President. Do we really want that?

In conclusion, we do NOT need more violence in the nation. There is already too much violence! Violence in movies and some TV shows propagate violence. I once make a statement to my aunt when she was screaming angrily at her son. My statement was "violence begets violence." Many years later, she reminded me that I had made that statement. So it is with disrespect. The disrespect at our Nation's Capital on January 6, 2021 only spawned more disrespect. I refer the reader to my book Happiness is the Truth, article 8 entitled "Where Has the Respect Gone?" Disrespect of our nation's institutions, especially the right to hold fair elections where everyone's vote is counted as much as our poll workers can accomplish. "Mail in ballots" should count too. We mail lots of stuff today. And, the mail receptacles where ballots are mailed should be reasonably near where people live so that they can walk to them if they lack transportation. Trump felt cheated when he was ahead in Georgia in the last election when he found the votes were turning against him. I was a postal worker for 22 years and certainly realize that it takes time for the mail to be processed and delivered to the polling sites. Was Trump so uninformed that he did not realize that mail-in ballots are not e-mails? The mail-in ballots took time to be sorted and delivered through the United States Postal Service to the polling sites. So, the mail-in-ballots were counted later than in-person ballots. Poor Blacks voted much more than Whites for Biden, particularly in Metropolitan Atlanta, Georgia. Thus, the victory for Biden with the mail-in ballots. Our great nation does NOT need someone who has rash judgement and is voted out due to mail-in ballots from poor Blacks who lacked transportation to the polling sites, so they deposited their ballots in the "drop boxes" found closer to their homes than the polling sites. I rest my case.

15
What was the Purpose of the Reported Apparitions of St. Mary?

Here are the visions of St. Mary that have been reported:

1. 1531:   Our Lady of Guadeloupe to Indian (Native) Juan Diego in Mexico
2. 1858:   Our Lady of Lourdes in France
3. 1859:   Our Lady (Shrine of God Help Us) by Adele Brise in Champion, Wisconsin
4. 1917:   Our Lady of Fatima (Portugal)
5. 1917:   Our Lady of Medjugorje
6.   Recent Vision of St. Mary near Necedah, Wisconsin

Our Lady of Guadeloupe appeared to Native Mexican children when they were being conquered by the

Spaniards: killed and tortured. Also, the Native persons suffered from disease brought by the Spaniards.

Our Lady of Lourdes was meant to bring healing of illnesses through healing water. A place of Hope.

Our Lady (Shrine of God Help Us) near Champion, Wisconsin in 1859 occurred just two years before the start of the US Civil War. Thus the connection to help us in wartime. It was officially recognized by the Bishop of Green Bay, Wisconsin, the only US apparition to be recognized by the Catholic Church.

Mary, the Mother of Jesus appeared to children in the Twentieth Century. It was at Fatima, Portugal the same year (1917) that the Bolshevik Revolution occurred when the early Marxists, which are today commonly known as Communists, overthrew the Russian Czar. It was reported that one of the children who received knowledge from Mary gave her a letter, not to be opened until a much later date (1968) by that child who became a Catholic nun. When that nun—Lucia—had her letter opened, it read "Russia will spread her errors throughout the entire world, fomenting war and persecution of the Church", so pray for the conversion of Russia. Fast forward to today, with the Russian invasion of Ukraine. Another message from Fatima read something like "the pope will suffer much" referring to the assassination attempt on Pope John Paul II on May 13, 1981. Later, that same Pope "heard" the confession of the man who shot him. Isn't such forgiveness rare? (The reader should note that I have witnesses Black women forgiving a person who killed one of her children. It was televised. Discrimination against GOODNESS is NEVER acceptable! It is WRONG! Some Blacks are Exceptionally GOOD!). Pope John Paul II was canonized on 27 April 2014, Saint Peter's Square, Vatican City by Pope Francis.

Another possible apparition occurred in, Medjugorje. a village in the south of Bosnia and Herzegovina. In December 7, 2017, it was reported that Archbishop Hoser, Pope Francis' envoy to Medjugorje announced that official Pilgrimages are allowed. The Holy See officially approved such Pilgrimages. However, this approval was not to signify recognition of the apparitions, but acknowledges the faith and pastoral needs of pilgrims. (Wikipedia). The reader should note that the former Yugoslavia had a civil war commonly known as the Yugoslav Wars. Ethnic tensions were suppressed by an autocratic government at this time. (1990s). Thus, Mary appeared after the war in that area of the world.

In the early 1970s I did visit a shrine near Necedah, Wisconsin where Mary supposedly appeared., However, I have not found it to be recognized yet by the Catholic Church. My understanding of that vision is the "roses from heaven fell down from the sky". At the shrine was a large crucifix with an image of the Christ cut up with which appeared to be knives all over His body. It appeared to be "overdone", but we really do not know for sure what happened at His Crucifixion.

In conclusion, my interpretation of the apparitions of St. Mary is that she appeared in a time of need with encouragement to pray to her, particularly to pray the Rosary. Her apparitions are meant to give hope in times of distress (war time) or to give healing. (Lourdes, France).

16
Inclusiveness: Transgender, facial rings, and tattoos

My message about Transgender is this: have compassion for those who have tried to change their sex with hormones and/or surgery. I do not believe such persons are happy. I met a young transgender man who wanted to become a woman. He was very unhappy. Think of it—having his genitals cut off with surgery hoping to find his "real" sexual identity. Such surgery is painful and permanent. Besides, he will never forget he was born a male or female.

Let's be satisfied with what God gave us. DO NOT, I repeat, DO NOT encourage transgender medical procedures. It is downright SINFUL! But, do not discriminate nor condemn those who do it. We are all sinners, so pray for them! Jesus came to save the world, not condemn it. Read article 50, Love and Inspiration, Not Judgement and Condemnation in my book God is the Truth.

In conclusion, be optimistic about what God gave us rather than complaining about it. God made us just exactly as He wanted us. (Except, of course, some procedures to correct birth defects are OK and even virtuous to improve the appearance and happiness of a person. But most persons should be satisfied with the way God made them). The same could be said about "fake" piercings and tattoos. Beauty is only "skin deep". Why ruin the beauty of the human body with rings in our noses or other parts of our face and/or tattoos? Tattoos can appear temporarily beautiful if done professionally. However, they are almost absolutely permanent and FADE over time, when they become very unattractive. Some persons put important messages in tattoos, such as Biblical writings. I must defend such "advertising" of Holy Scripture if one is willing to accept the ugliness when those tattoos fade too. However, it is better to promote Scripture with talk rather than an outward sign on your beautiful body. But never cruelly criticize or judge someone suffering from an ugly tattoo. Love is Kind. (St, Paul in his letter to the Corinthians).

Turning to "fake" piercings in the nose or other parts of the face, such additions tend to ruin the natural beauty of the face. Ear rings are traditionally more acceptable and do not interfere with breathing or a "runny nose", when one must remove the ring. Read article 49, Beauty in Life of my book God is the Truth. But, remember such behaviors are not sinful, just unnecessary and can ruin an already beautiful body. But, do not discriminate against such persons who do such superficial things to their bodies. Such activities were and still are a "fad". My parents told us NOT to follow the crowd. My dad said: "If most others were jumping in the lake, that doesn't mean we have to do it too". Be an individual to "stand out from the crowd" if that is what it takes to be your "true self". Also, heavy facial "make-up" (cosmetics) like too much eye shadow or extended "fake" eye lashes are often detrimental to beauty. To me, it makes one less attractive. Moderation is the key. (I do not include make-up to cover wrinkles in this category. Their use is certainly acceptable. However, sunblock before sun exposure to prevent skin damage from sunburn is better, especially if one is "fair skinned". But creams and oils can still be used to at least partially heal sunburn or skin damage from over exposure to water or very dry air).

17
Jesus: His Yoke is Light

Thank you, Jesus, for paving the way for me so that I need NOT suffer like you did for me and for all of mankind. Your yoke was and still is easy because you beat Satan and showed us how to beat Satan too. Your Love for your Father, Mother and Holy Spirit as well as for mankind beat Satan. Our love for God above all and others as ourselves is our clear path to victory over Satan and an easy yoke, because it is accepting your yoke.

"Come to me all you that are weary and carrying heavy burdens, and I will give you rest. Take my yoke upon you, and learn from me, for I am gentle and humble in heart, and you will find rest for your souls. For my yoke is easy and my burden is light". Matthew 11:28-30. Refer to my book God is Love, article 15: A Crisis in Faith and a Spiritual Awakening.

18
Life is Love

Without Love, Life is NOT worth living. Love is what makes life worthwhile. St Paul said "without love, I am nothing—just a gonging cymbal—just noise".

Jesus loves all of us without exception. We should listen to His word in Scripture when he tells us what He can do for us. "Come to me all you who are weary and heavy burdened and I will give you rest…I am gentle and humble of heart." Matthew 11: 28-29.

Jesus offered not only "Everlasting Life", but also "Peace"— "Peace the world cannot give." (Refer to my book—Is God Peace.)

19
Gun Control

There are those that say if we have gun control, only criminals will have guns. Sure, let's have no gun control and criminals will be free to use military style assault weapons, machine guns, to randomly kill many persons in one swipe. Is that what we want?

Another argument is that our right to bear arms is guaranteed by the 2nd Amendment. Yes, to protect us citizens against tyranny, such as a dictatorial government which wishes to control its citizens UNJUSTLY with weapons or guns. Such a government is Communistic. Donald Trump's
 actions and friendship Putin suggest he may think communism is an acceptable alternative to democracy. He declared he could end the war in Ukraine in One day. Of course he could. He would stop all our US military efforts to protect Ukraine from Russia and let Russia take Ukraine. Seems simple enough to me.

Another argument is that people kill people, not guns. Really, what happens if one of those persons uses a gun to kill someone rather than a fist? Which weapon is more likely to kill another person. All weapons that are part of the body are less lethal than guns or even clubs. In my military service, we were taught to call our guns "weapons". Military weapons are used now including bombs and missiles from planes, submarines or other launching systems, because this is Not Utopia. If such military weapons are used to save the lives of our (USA) allies for national defense, such use is OK. But, only if our Goals of using such weapons are likely attainable. Can we win the war? (Unlike Vietnam where we're unlikely to win and actually LOST. Refer to article 11 Sweet Cherry Wine in this book. That unjust war needlessly cost many lives.

In conclusion let's have sensible GUN CONTROL to prevent many needless deaths. JUSTICE REQUIRES GUN CONTROL. GOD IS JUSTICE! AMEN!

God Loves All Of US. Please accept HIS Love to be Saved!

*Michael John DeNucci lives in Cumberland, WI
and is a freelance writer for God and Mankind*

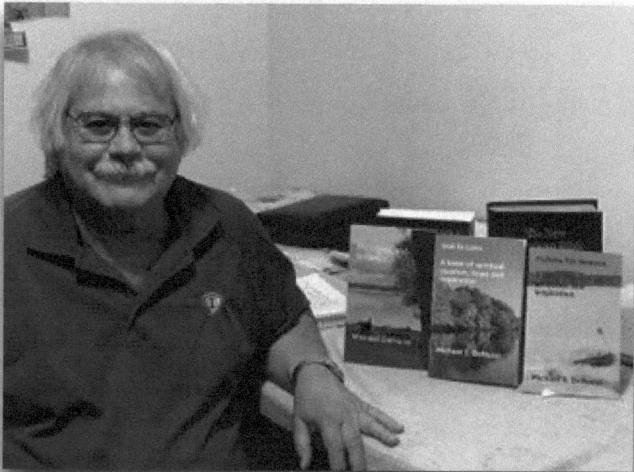

Michael John DeNucci attended his first two years of high school at Holy Cross Seminary in Lacrosse, Wisconsin and then returned to graduate from Cumberland High School. He went on to earn his Bachelor's Degree in Political Science from the College of St Thomas in St Paul, Minnesota, attended the University of Wisconsin at Madison partially completing an MBA, and then earning a Master's Degree in Industrial Relations from the University of Minnesota. He is an Army Veteran who has served stateside and in Germany. He has held a variety of jobs over his lifetime which have broadened his perspectives on the relationship of God and Mankind.

Other Books by Michael John DeNucci

"Thoughts and Writings"

"Fishing for Heaven"

"God is Love"

"Is God Happiness"

"Is Love the Truth"

"Happiness is the Truth"

"Is God Freedom?"

"Is Love Freedom"

"Is God Mercy"

"Is God Peace?"

"God is the Truth"